# FREE MASK

## You Will Need:

- Thin elastic, wool or string

- Scissors

- Sticky Tape

## Instructions:

1. Pull out the mask page.
2. Pop out the mask.
3. Cut enough elastic/wool/string to fit around the back of your head.
4. Attach to the back of the mask with some sticky tape.
5. Have fun with your new mask!

**SCISSORS ARE SHARP! ASK AN ADULT FOR HELP BEFORE USING.**

# WE LOVE 1D

## By Sarah Palmer

Published 2014.

Pedigree Books Limited, Beech Hill House,
Walnut Gardens, Exeter, Devon EX4 4DH

www.pedigreebooks.com | books@pedigreegroup.co.uk

ISBN 9781908152497

# Contents

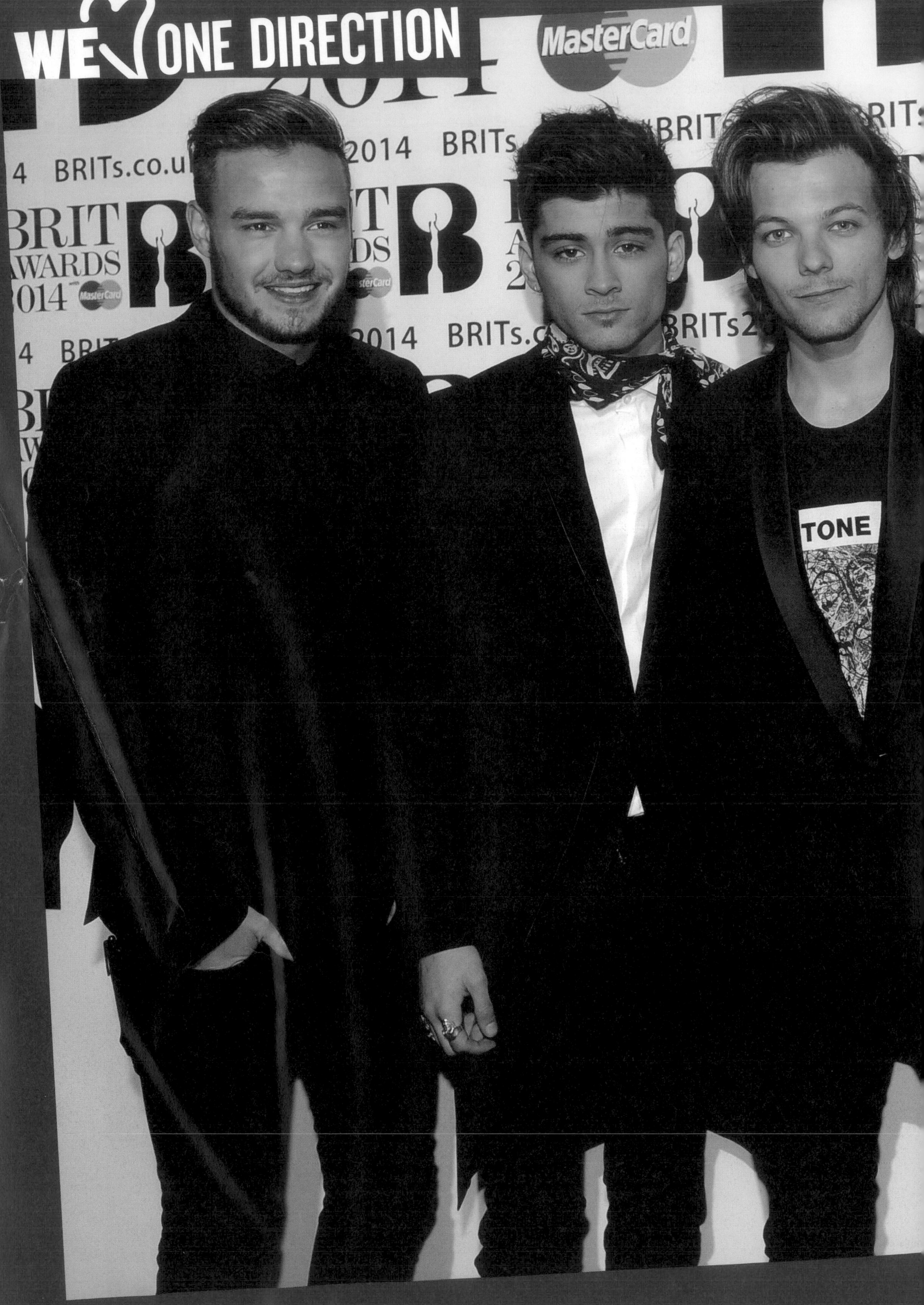
MasterCard
BRIT
AWARDS
2014
MasterCard
TONE

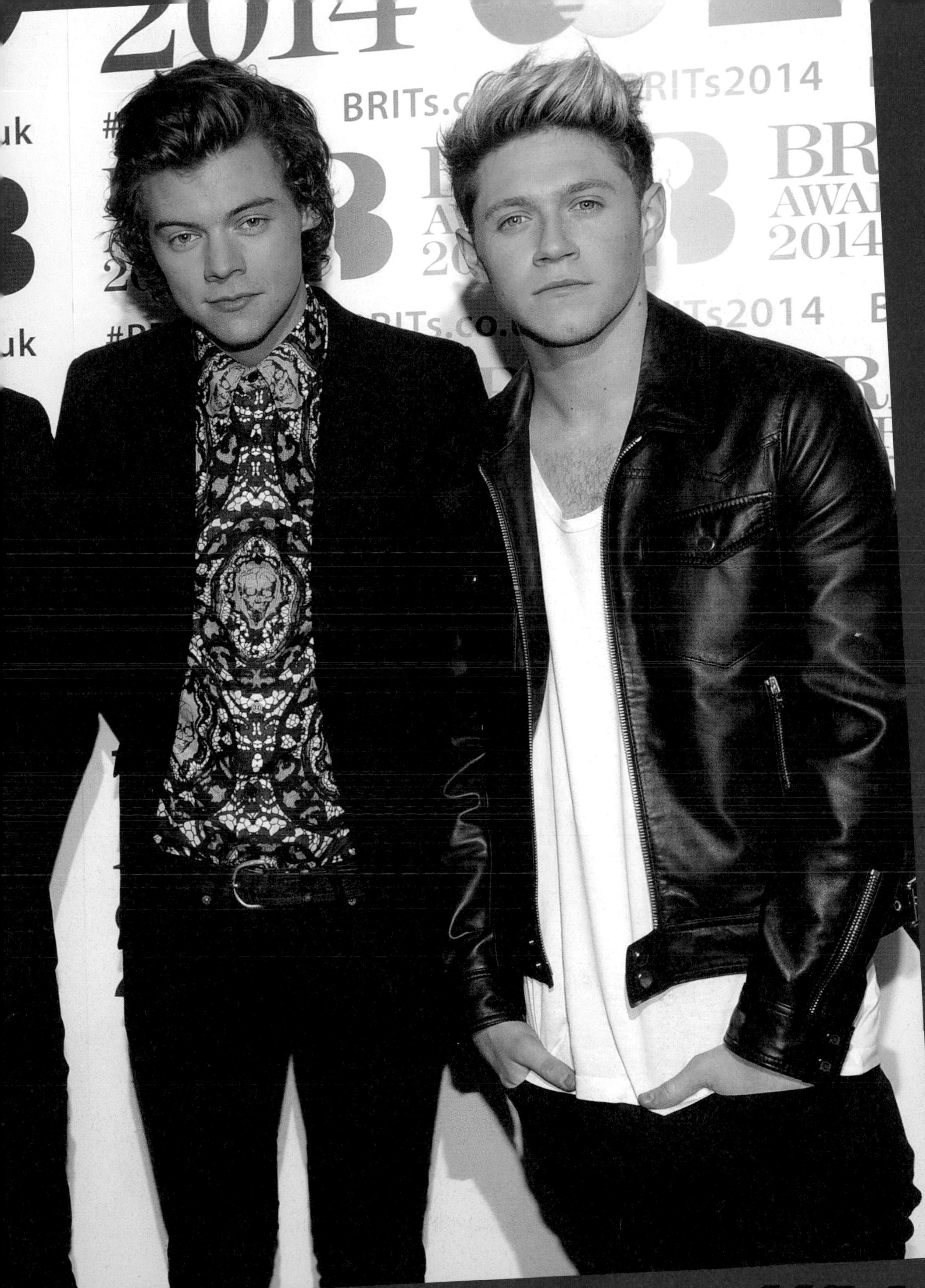

smash hits!

# NEED TO KNOW

THE BIG FACTS ALL FANS SHOULD KNOW ABOUT THEIR NO.1 BOY!

**What do his mates call him?**
Hazza

**How random!** Haz says the scariest thing he has ever done is make a speech at his mum's wedding. Also one of his heroes is none other than David "The Hoff" Hasselhoff.

**Thumbs up!** Harry has crushes on lots of ladies (especially ones who make him laugh) including Jennifer Lawrence and Rihanna. Music wise he likes Adele, Ed Sheeran and Coldplay, and cats are his favourite animals.

Harry loves amazing Adele

He's a mayo-free zone

**Thumbs down...** Don't try to feed Harry mayonnaise – he hates it! He's also not a fan of swearing or people being rude, and reckons his biggest fault is that he tends to fall asleep at every opportunity.

**Awww, bless!**
Harry is such a mummy's boy he'll call his ma Anne up to five times a day. She says, "When there's a time difference, he tends to text saying, 'I love you, Mum,' or 'I miss you'. He's still my little boy." Sob.

Hazza hearts his mum

# NEED TO KNOW

**THE BIG FACTS ALL FANS SHOULD KNOW ABOUT THEIR NO.1 BOY!**

**What do his mates call him?**
Lou Boo Bear

**How random!** Louis likes girls who are fond of carrots. He once pulled down Niall's pants at a petrol station for a laugh, and when he was at school he flashed his bum at the headteacher.

Louis' crush Emma Watson

**Thumbs up!** Louis fancies Emma Watson, has a talent for doing silly voices and his favourite food is macaroni cheese. Or in fact, anything with cheese!

**Thumbs down...** He bites his nails and doesn't like smokers, baked beans and people who makes loads of noise when they eat. Who does?

No baked beans, please

**Erm, excuse us?** Louis may have four best mates in the other 1D boys but he's keen to have a pal of the hairier variety. "I'd like to adopt a chimpanzee and build an eternal friendship, that would be amazing," he says. Perfectly normal.

Louis would like to monkey around

# NEED TO KNOW

THE BIG FACTS ALL FANS SHOULD KNOW ABOUT THEIR NO.1 BOY!

**What do his mates call him?** Zaynster

**How random!** Zayn didn't even have a passport when he first joined 1D and has never learned to swim. He also held Harry's hand when he was getting his first tattoo. Aww!

**Thumbs up!** Girls wise, Zayn only has eyes for his gorgeous other half, Perrie from Little Mix. He rates superstar Justin Timblerlake, loves drawing and you may have noticed he's a bit of a tattoo fan?

Lovely Perrie

Zayn: not a fan of pyjamas

**Thumbs down...** Zayn is open about the fact he's pretty vain and says it's sometimes his downfall. He avoids sandwich crusts, heights (he hates 'em) and pyjamas (they're too hot apparently!).

**Geek chic!** Zayn may be super-cool but he admits to having one very geeky habit – he's obsessed with comic books and used to collect loads of them when he was a kid.

Zayn loves a good comic

# NEED TO KNOW

**THE BIG FACTS ALL FANS SHOULD KNOW ABOUT THEIR NO.1 BOY!**

**What do his mates call him?** Paynee

**How random!** Liam has a fear of getting old and wrinkly (you're OK for a while, Paynee!), and his sister Ruth has over 900,000 followers on Twitter. Wowsers.

Liam thinks Selena's hot

**Thumbs up!** Surfing is Liam's favourite way to chill out. He also likes chocolate, his curly hair and anything to do with Disney. Bless! Oh, and he's also got a crush on Selena Gomez.

**Thumbs down...** Liam reckons he worries too much, and doesn't like show-offs, flying or a certain round-shaped member of the cutlery family (spoons, if you haven't worked it out).

Keep those spoons away!

**He's our hero!** Liam dramatically saved his friend Andy Samuels when he was filling up Liam's patio heater in 2013. Andy was seriously injured, but it would have been much worse if Liam hadn't intervened. In fact, Liam once wanted to be a firefighter!

We'd like to see Liam in uniform

# NEED TO KNOW

**What do his mates call him?**
Nialler

**How random!** He went to his first gig in Dublin at the age of ten - to see Busted. When things get awkward, Niall has been known to say, "cheeseburgers and jelly babies!" Er, OK, Nialler.

**Thumbs up!** Niall's crush is Demi Lovato and the Victoria's Secret Angels models (we wonder why?), he loves the film Grease and his top singer is Michael Bublé. He's also a massive Bon Jovi fan.

Niall's crush Demi

No clowning around for Niall

**Thumbs down...** Niall has a fear of birds flying around inside, wouldn't ever go to a circus (because he hates clowns) and admits his worst habit is farting. Ewwww!

**Lol!** We all know it was Harry who came up with the name One Direction but if Niall had got his way they would have been called something else altogether. His suggestion? Erm, Niall And The Potatoes. Catchy.

Anyone for Niall And The Potatoes?

# WHOSE TAT
## CAN YOU MATCH THE TATTOO

# S THAT?

## O THE INKED-UP ID MEMBER?

**HOW WELL DO YOU KNOW THE BOYS' BODS?**

1. ......................
2. ......................
3. ......................
4. ......................
5. ......................
6. ......................
7. ......................
8. ......................
9. ......................
10. ......................

# 1D: How It All Went So Right!

## They've become the biggest band in the universe, but just how did they manage it?

Way back in 2010, five solo artists decided to follow their dreams of musical stardom and audition for The X Factor. Liam, Harry, Niall, Louis and Zayn all got through to Bootcamp, but were devastated when they were told that it was the end of the road and they wouldn't be going on to Judges' Houses. But little did they know that a secret plan was being hatched...

Simon Cowell, Nicole Sherzinger and Louis Walsh put their heads together and decided to let the lads try out again, but this time as a band. The five-piece soon became One Direction and they zoomed through Judges' Houses to land a place in the live finals, eventually coming third in the competition. They were snapped up by Simon Cowell's record label Syco and headed to LA and Sweden to record their debut album.

Their first single, 'What Makes You Beautiful', was released in September 2011 and went straight to number one in the UK and Ireland. After releasing their second single 'It's Gotta Be You', the boys were truly established and headed out on their first ever headline tour.

In February 2012, the guys won an esteemed BRIT award for Best British Single for 'What Makes You Beautiful'.

America came calling and 1D were offered a megabucks record deal across the pond, and the US soon fell as head over heels in love with them as the rest of us.

They released their second album, 'Take Me Home', in the summer of 2012, which provided them with a number one smash around the world.

Later that year the five-piece announced they were set to release a behind the scenes DVD about life in 1D, and were also embarking on a huge world tour in 2013. They soon snagged another BRIT award (this time for Global success) and started work on their third album.

The first One Direction movie, 'This Is Us', was released in August 2013 and topped the box office across the globe. Album number three, 'Midnight Memories', was another huge hit when it was unleashed in November 2013.

In February 2014 the guys were presented with their third BRIT award, for Global Success, and fourth, for Best British Video for 'Best Song Ever'. They also announced another world tour, and spoke of plans to work on a fourth album (squeal!). As for the future? It couldn't be brighter!

The lads are now the most successful band in the entire world!

1D always like to give the fans a glimpse of them!

Harry and Co. are always appearing on chat shows

productions

AN MUSIC AW

MUSIC

EARLY PICS

2

**3**

**1**

**4**

**5**

**1** We're glad that the lads don't share the same jackets any more!

**2** We can't get over how young the boys look here

**3** You wouldn't catch them in a onesie in public these days

**4** The lads were posing pros from the word go

**5** Remember Louis' stripes phase? He loved 'em!

# WHICH *1D* BOY IS YOUR PERFECT MATCH?

**Always wondered which 1D boy you should date? Our cunning quiz will reveal all!**

**The 1D boy of your dreams is taking you on a date! Where do you want them to take you?**

A The cinema
B A comedy night
C An art exhibition
D A cool party
E A lovely restaurant

**What would you like your 1D boyfriend to buy you for your birthday?**

A A Playstation game
B A One Direction DVD for a joke!
C A cute dress
D A day trip to Paris
E A huge cuddly bear

**How would you spend your perfect day off?**

A Chilling out in front of the TV
B Playing sports with your mates
C Seeing your family
D Shopping with pals and flashing the cash
E Hanging out with the object of your affection

**What's the first thing you do in the morning?**

A Jump in the shower
B Watch something silly on YouTube
C Tweet a good morning message to everyone
D Wish you could go back to sleep
E Think about what you're going to wear

## What last made you cry?
A Something sad you saw on the news
B You actually cried laughing at something
C Missing friends or family
D A romantic film
E Everything makes you cry. You're pretty sensitive!

## How would your friends describe you?
A Serious at times, but you know how to have fun
B Funny and a bit hyperactive
C Sensitive and kind
D Chilled-out and happy
E Good fun but a bit of a worrier

## How would you describe your style?
A Cute and girlie
B Sporty and laid back
C Feminine with an edge
D Super trendy
E Simple and sophisticated

**Mostly As – Liam** You and Liam are a match made in heaven

**Mostly Bs – Niall** You're laid back and fun-loving just like Niall

**Mostly Cs – Zayn** You and Zayn would be a perfect pairing

**Mostly Ds Harry** You and Harry would fall in L-O-V-E!

**Mostly Es – Louis** It could be wedding bells for you and Louis

# Tweet Treats!

Harry and Co. love having their say on Twitter.
Here are some of their best tweets and pics!

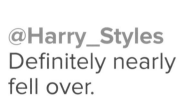

**@Louis_ Tomlinson** Screen debut for the grandparents haha! Love it!!

**@Harry_Styles** Definitely nearly fell over.

**@Real_Liam_Payne** Sundays are really boring.

@Zaynmalik

**@Harry_Styles** @5SOS love the new video emos!! Makes me wanna throw clothes at you.

**@Real_Liam_ Payne** Right last night was so crazyyyyy, which always leads to a crazy dream... Playing table tennis with jay z was on the mind not sure why :/???

**@NiallOfficial** One of them ones where ya don't know what you want for lunch!! #niallerproblems.

**@Harry_Styles** Unidentified gel in deceivingly small tube does not taste the same as toothpaste. Fact.

**@NiallOfficial** So tired I'm just gona chill for the day! Probs fall asleep on the couch!

**@Harry_Styles** Eating toast in the shower is the ultimate multitask.

**@Louis_ Tomlinson** You guys really have been so amazing over these few weeks :) loads of love :)

**@NiallOfficial** Too early to be waking up, gotta be done!

**@Louis_Tomlinson** Dairy Milk Oreo is the best chocolate since Dairy Milk biscuit! Amazing!

**@Zaynmalik** Sometimes you pretend even when it's real ...x

**@Real_Liam_Payne** Loving the den right now great vibe great night for a pants day.

**@Zaynmalik** I'll give but if there's nothing left to give what can I do??,,,,,,,,,,

**@Zaynmalik** Sometimes just the sound of someone's voice can make you happy :D x

**@Louis_ Tomlinson** So our next single is gonna be Story of My Life.

**@Real_ Liam_Payne** Hello mr @ scott_mills listenin to you far away on holiday thank you for providing the soundtrack to our beach view.

**@Louis_ Tomlinson** Wow I just make typos all day long.

**@NiallOfficial** I would like to thank@British Monarchy and of course queen Elizabeth for her invite to Buckingham palace yesterday evening.

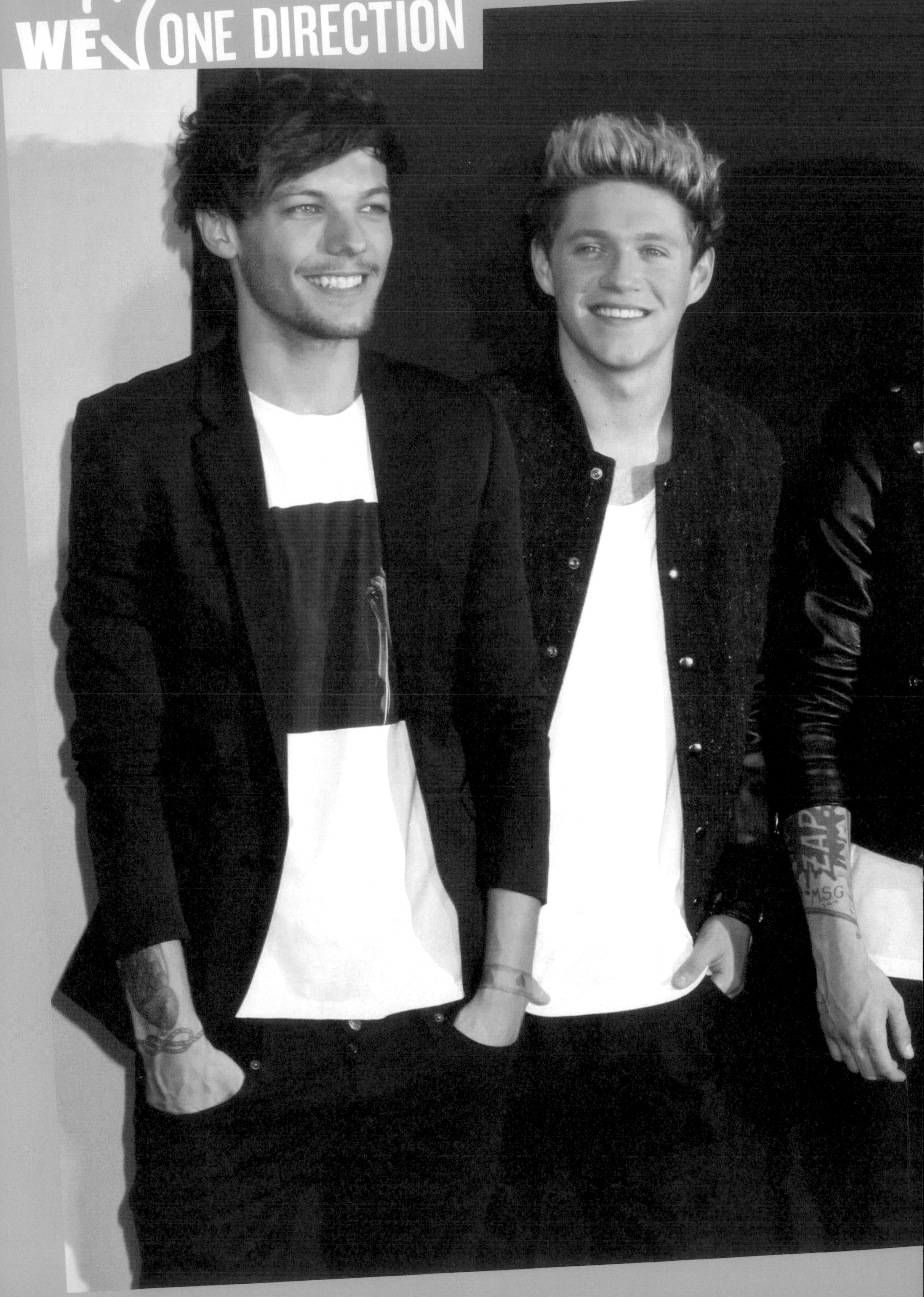

# SUPER STATS!

The boys keep getting bigger –
and so do their amazing stats

## Over 85 million singles and albums sold worldwide

## A NO.1 MOVIE IN THE UK AND USA

## 94 No.1 worldwide singles and albums

## 3 huge albums

## 11 MASSIVE HIT SINGLES

## Three sell-out world tours

SON
make.be

# Over 20 million Facebook fans

**Over 80 million Twitter followers between them**

## THREE UK NUMBER ONE SINGLES

Tickets for the band's Madison Square Gardens concert sold out **in 10 minutes!**

**Over 58 million Google searches in ONE year**

Even Harry has dodgy face days!

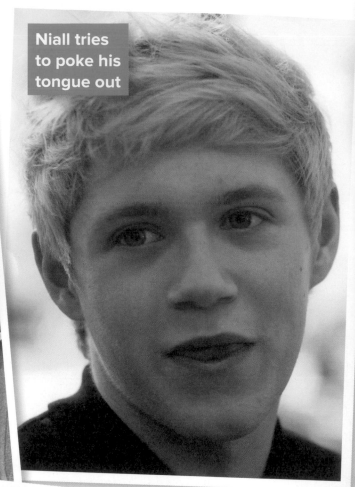

Niall tries to poke his tongue out

# FUNNY FACES

They may be gorgeous but 1D don't mind pulling faces from time to time!

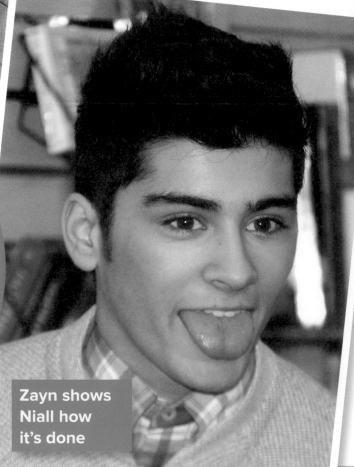

Zayn shows Niall how it's done

Let's hope the wind doesn't change, Harry!

Zayn's just seen his new hair!

Louis gets so excited when it rains

Liam's also just seen Zayn's new hair...

# CRACKING QUOTES

1D are ace. Fact. Here are some of their best musings

**"When I was little, I always wanted a brother, and now it's like I've got four of them."**
**Liam**

"Personally I wouldn't like to be food because I wouldn't like to be eaten."
**Niall**

"Live for who you are and what you love."
**Zayn**

"Who doesn't need an eraser? Everyone makes mistakes."
**Louis**

**"The strongest people aren't always the people who win, but the people who don't give up when they lose."**
**Liam**

"Every day should be a new day."
**Harry**

"Without the fans, there is no reason to be One Direction!"
**Zayn**

"When Zayn is tired, he won't care who you are, he will sleep on your shoulder."
**Liam**

"Harry loves to steal food off people's plates, but he is too scared to do it to Niall."
Louis

**"If it were legal, I'd marry food."**
Niall

"Stop worrying about someone that isn't worried about you. Never leave your key of happiness in someone else's pockets."
**Zayn**

**"Live life to the fullest because everything else is uncertain."**
Louis

"Believe it or not, but even when I'm sleeping, I'm dreaming about meeting fans."
**Liam**

**"If I was in a horror film I'd die first, because I would have no idea what's going on."**
Niall

**"There comes a day when you realise turning the page is the best feeling in the world, because you realise there's so much more to the book than the page you were stuck on."**
Zayn

**"I drew a cat recently and Louis asked me why I was drawing a giraffe."**
Harry

**"Signing my first autograph was quite awkward because I didn't have one."**
Harry

"My favourite one in the group was Zayn, until he stole my meal. Now Harry is my favourite."
Niall

**"We're not perfect, we're not clean cut. We're just trying to be ourselves."**
Louis

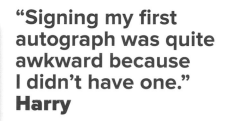

WE ♥ ONE DIRECTION

smashhits!

# How To Date

**1** You don't have to go OTT to pull 1D. In fact, Harry says he prefers a low-key lady. "A short skirt and lots of make-up won't impress me," he admits. He also likes a girl with brains, and jokes: "I'd kill for a super-intelligent girlfriend."

**2** Niall agrees with Harry and reckons love isn't about looks. "I'm the kind of boy that can fall in love with any girl because I love with the heart, not the eyes," he says. So cute! When it comes to what kind of girls he likes, Niall isn't after a supermodel type. "Anyone who is funny and doesn't take herself too seriously is attractive to me."

**3** Harry doesn't go in for perfection either, saying: "A real girl is perfect, and a perfect girl isn't real."

**4** You can expect some serious romance if you date Liam. "Love is all about communication, so we'd go hand-in-hand on a romantic stroll through the park and I'd buy her flowers." Liam also admits: "I'm a massive softy." Plenty of chocs and cuddly toys all round, then.

**5** Harry's best love advice? Don't worry about what other people think of the object of your affection. "Don't choose the one who is beautiful to the world. But rather choose the one who makes your world beautiful."

**6** Louis sounds like the perfect bf. "I'm a very loyal boyfriend. I'm a bit of a joker... I can be romantic, but not too sickly." Sadly he's also super-dedicated to his long-term girlfriend Eleanor Calder. "Every night before I go to sleep, I always talk to my girlfriend Eleanor," Louis reveals.

**7** Zayn likes girls who are independent but he also loves to look after his lady and says: "If my girlfriend needs anything, I'm always here for her." Zayn also reckons that just because you're single, you shouldn't feel anything less than amazing. "Just because you don't have a prince does not mean you are not a princess." And just when we thought we couldn't fall for Zayn any more he goes and says: "Don't ever let a guy make you feel ugly because no matter what, you are beautiful with or without him."

**8** And here's something you can look forward to if you snare Niall. "I give great hugs!" You know where we are, Nialler... Niall admits he would love to squeeze all of the Directioners if he could. "If our fans only know how badly I want to meet and hug them!" he laughs. Maybe Niall could give Harry a hug? The poor boy has admitted: "I wish I had a girl to cuddle up to at night instead of my pillow!"

**9** Finally, take some sound advice from wise Zayn who reckons: "You've got to take risks to find love." We'd risk pretty much anything to go on a romantic meal with any of the guys!

# 1D

Fancy having a member of 1D as your boyfriend? Then you need to know what they look for in a lady!

# WHO SAID WHAT?

Can you match these brilliant quotes to the right band member?

**1.** "Life is a funny thing. The minute you think you've got everything figured out, something comes along and turns it upside down."

**2.** "My sister used to call me Cheesy-Head because I loved these cheesy crisps."

**3.** "I don't think you can really define love."

**4.** "I like girls who eat carrots."

**5.** "I'll always defend the people I love."

**6.** "I once cried in a restaurant because the waitress told me I couldn't eat my soup with a fork, I had to use a spoon."

**7.** "Sometimes we have such long days and we just need to be stupid to get through them."

9. "And remember people: you might not be plastic, but you are fantastic!"

8. "If a man whistles at you, don't turn around, ignore him. You're lady, not a dog."

10. "If you want to go somewhere, you can do it. Nothing is stopping you."

12. "There comes a day when you realise turning the page is the best feeling in the world."

11. "The worst thing a guy could do to a girl? Personally I think it's to ignore her while she's loving you with all her heart."

13. "Once we went eight hours without eating, so Louis took out a cereal bar, and instead of eating it, he gave it to me."

14. "My trademark saying is probably 'VAS HAPPENIN?!'"

ANSWERS: 1 ZAYN 2 LIAM 3 HARRY 4 LOUIS 5 NIALL 6 LIAM 7 HARRY 8 NIALL 9 LOUIS 10 LOUIS 11 LIAM 12 ZAYN 13 NIALL 14 ZAYN

Harry loves a free bag...

... but not as much as Niall does!

# PAPPED!

Those boys just can't go anywhere without being caught on camera!

If you can't beat them join them, Mr Styles

Louis likes to show off his arms in pics!

Liam has perfected his cool camera face

# Fab Faves

Here are a few of 1D's favourite things!

GLASSES

## Harry

Harry's fragrance of choice? **Diesel Fuel For Life**

Harry says that **eating nachos** makes him happy!

Harry loves his **gorgeous curls** and has nightmares about people trying to straighten them

**Tattoos.** You may have noticed that all of the boys (apart from Niall) rather like them...

## Louis

**Hollister aftershave.** We bet he smells amaze

Louis often rocks a pair of **glasses** because he likes the geek-chic look

Louis has watched all of the **Twilight films** numerous times and is a dedicated Twihard

TWILIGHT

**Doncaster Rovers Football Club.** Louis is so dedicated he's even brought the club!

Louis dreams of appearing on **EastEnders** one day

TATtOOS

DRFC

LAUGHING!

JOHN MAYER

MARVIN & ROCHELLE

# Zayn

**Justin Timberlake.** He's one of Zayn's biggest idols and he really hopes to work with him one day. He's even a fan of Justin's old band, *NSync

Zayn hopes to become an actor one day and also spends a lot of his spare time **drawing** as he's a brilliant artist

**Laughing.** The gang never stop – they make each other crack up constantly. They make us laugh all the time too!

# Liam

Liam loves **showers** as he reckons they get him ready for a hard day's work

**John Mayer's music.** He's the guy who used to go out with Katy Perry, btw!

Liam is a big fan of singing superstar **Usher** and would love to work with him one day

USHER

# Niall

**Screaming.** Niall and Co. adore hearing all of their fans screaming, especially when they're at concerts

**Nando's and Wagamama** are two of Niall's top restaurants

Niall says **his guitar** is one of his most treasured possessions.

**Marvin and Rochelle Humes.** They're two of Nialler's best mates

**Twitter.** All of the lads love tweeting (see our feature on page 30!) so they can keep fans up to date with what they're up to

# FAMOUS FANS

It's not just us lot that love 1D. These famous faces can't get enough of them either!

**LITTLE MIX** It's no surprise that Little Mix and One Direction are top showbiz pals when Zayn is engaged to band member Perrie. They're all super-supportive of each other.

**TOM FLETCHER** The boys have worked with the McBusted singer in the recording studio and written with him loads of times. They've all become firm friends.

**JUSTIN BIEBER** Niall has made no secret of the fact that he's a massive Justin fan, and he was beyond excited to meet his idol. He's even been to Zayn's house for dinner.

**KATY PERRY** Katy first met Niall when she was a guest judge on The X Factor, and was partly responsible for him getting through to the next round of the comp.

**ROBBIE WILLIAMS** As a former boy bander himself, Robbie knows that it's like to be in a huge pop combo. He thinks the boys are ace and that Harry is amazing. He's once gushed: "He's beguiling, and so are One Direction."

**JOE JONAS** One third of the mighty Jonas Brothers reckons 1D are the business. "They are top boys. I love their songs, I'm glad I got to see them perform. They're huge!" he says.

# Spot The Difference

## Can you spot the five slightly obvious differences between these two pics of the boys below?

**ANSWERS ON PAGE 76**

# 1D Discography

The boys can't stop having huge UK hits!
Look at their amazing achievements so far

## Albums

**Up All Night** - 2011 - Number 2

**Take Me Home** - 2012 - Number 1

**Midnight Memories** - 2013 - Number 1

## Singles

### 2011

**What Makes You Beautiful** - Number 1

**Gotta Be You** - Number 3

**One Thing** - Number 9

### 2012

**Live While We're Young** - Number 3

**Little Things** - Number 1

**Kiss You** - Number 9

**One Way or Another (Teenage Kicks)** - Number 1

### 2013

**Best Song Ever** - Number 2

**Story Of My Life** - Number 2

**Midnight Memories** - Number 39

MIDNIGHT
MEMORIES

smash hits!

# I Love One Direction because...

Write down the many reasons you love the world's greatest boy band HERE!

My top 1D song is...

They make me laugh most when...

I would like to go on a date with...

My top 1D single is...

The funniest member of 1D is...

The best bit of 1D memorabilia I have is...

Their funniest moment ever is...

........................................................................................................

1D once made me shed a happy tear because...

........................................................................................................

If I met 1D I would tell them...

........................................................................................................

The best memory I have of the lads is...

........................................................................................................

My best friend's fave member is...

........................................................................................................

The last dream I had about the boys was...

........................................................................................................

I think...           is the best dressed

band member.

I was shocked when I heard that 1D...

If I could have any member of the group round for dinner it would be...

and I would cook...

The band's best video is...

The One Direction guy who has the best hair is...

I think the best 1D album is...

The moment I first fell in love with the band was...

# THE GIA 10

**1** What is the name of 1D's third album?

**2** What is Liam's middle name?

**3** Which band member is from Doncaster?

**4** Who has a massive fear of rollercoasters?

**5** What was the band's first number one?

**6** Who once planned to become a drama teacher?

**7** Which band member didn't own a passport before he joined 1D?

**8** Who was 1D's mentor on The X Factor?

**9** What is 1D's behind the scenes DVD called?

**10** Whose favourite film is Forrest Gump?

# NT QUIZ!

Think you're ID's biggest superfan? Then take our brilliant quiz to find out just how much you really know!

**11** What was the name of the band Harry was in at school?

**12** Who has an older brother called Greg?

**13** Which ID-er wears Diesel Fuel For Live aftershave?

**14** What did Zayn sing at his first ever X Factor audition?

**15** What are Liam's sisters called?

**16** Niall screamed when a certain celeb followed him on Twitter, but who was it?

**17** Who once very famously said he liked girls who eat carrots?

**18** Which ID Boy once worked in a bakery?

**19** Who is the youngest member of ID?

**20** What's Liam's dad's name?

**21** Which band member used to work in a cinema?

**22** How many BRIT awards have ID won?

**23** Where is Zayn from?

**24** Who is the only band member not to have a tattoo?

**25** Who once dated Taylor Swift?

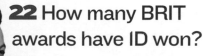

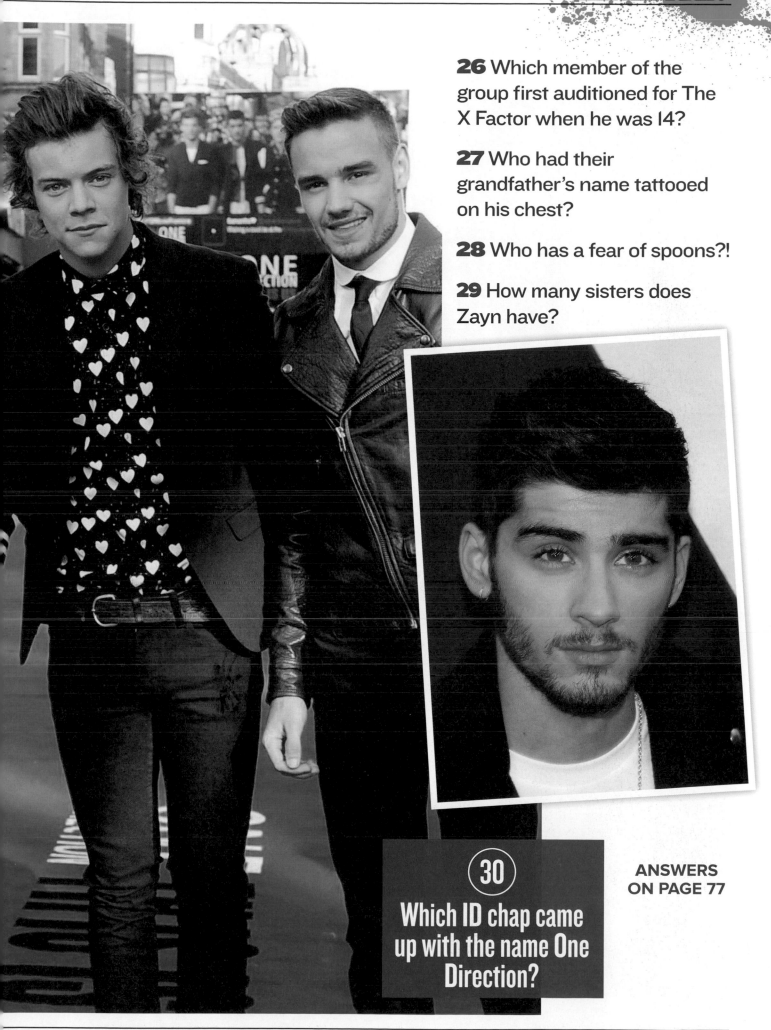

**26** Which member of the group first auditioned for The X Factor when he was 14?

**27** Who had their grandfather's name tattooed on his chest?

**28** Who has a fear of spoons?!

**29** How many sisters does Zayn have?

**30** Which 1D chap came up with the name One Direction?

ANSWERS ON PAGE 77

smashhits!

LIVE!

2

**1** The boys work super-hard to make sure they put on an amazing show for the fans

**2** Don't they get a bit hot in those jackets on stage?

**3** Yep, those T-shirts look much cooler, guys!

**4** Now THAT'S what we call co-ordinating

**5** Watch out for the falling phone boxes, fellas!

# WE ♥ 1D Because...

Let us count the reasons we love 1D! Oh, we can't, there are just too many...

**They're the world's best boy band. Fact.** They're one of the most successful groups of all time, and they just keep getting bigger and better!

**They're always having a laugh.** The fivesome love playing practical jokes on each other, and at one time they wanted their own prank show so they could also play tricks on unsuspecting members of the public!

**They're not afraid to big up other boy bands.** The guys are really good pals with 5 Seconds of Summer and are always tweeting their support for the four-piece.

**They're incredibly talented.** Not only do they sing beautifully, they also write as many of their songs as possible. They've all co-written tracks for the band and Harry has also written with Kodaline and OneRepublic. So clever!

**They're sensitive.** The boys are very open and honest about their feelings, and all admit they have times when things get a bit too much for them. Sensitive Niall even broke down when the band were recording the advert for their fragrance 'That Moment', and all the other lads raced to comfort him.

**They LOVE their fans.** They tweet as many of them as possible, and Harry once called up a lucky fan and left her a voicemail message. Er, here's our number, Hazza. You can call us anytime…

**They have the best hair ever.** From Louis' cool quiff to Harry's cute curls, the boys' locks always look amazing and they love experimenting with new looks.

**They're bang on trend.** Liam and Co. always look well turned out in the latest togs and they certainly know how to dress up for an important do. Have men ever looked hotter in a tuxedo?

**They still get starstruck.** Niall famously screamed when Justin Bieber followed him on Twitter, and got so excited when he met his footballing idol David Beckham, he turned to jelly.

**Their songs rock our world.** Every one of their singles to date have been 100% brilliant, and their albums are packed full of tracks we can dance, cry and sing along to.

# 1D AROUND THE WORLD!

World famous? Yep!

It's not just us lot in Blighty that love the boys, check out how well they're doing in the rest of the world!

✈ **America LOVES 1D! Amazingly One Direction are the first band in the history of the US Billboard 200 to have their first three albums go straight to number one.**

✈ The band are so big around the world they've scooped two Global Success BRIT awards.

✈ **1D's second album, 'Take Me Home' went to number one in a massive 37 countries and has sold over 5 million copies so far!**

✈ The boys adore Oz and it's where Liam and Louis learnt to surf.

✈ **The lads' third album, 'Midnight Memories' was** the fastest and biggest selling album of 2013 in the WORLD, and went to number one in 31 countries.

✈ Their sell-out 'Take Me Home' tour saw them visit Europe, America, Canada, Mexico, Australia, New Zealand and Japan.

✈ **The band have won 6 Teen Choice Awards in the US of A.**

✈ Up All Night: The Live Tour DVD was accredited 6 x platinum after just one week of release in Australia.

✈ **The guys have learnt some Japanese phrases so they can talk to their fans out there!**

✈ Harry is such a fan of France he once tweeted "J'adore la France." (which means he loves it!)

✈ **The boys performed 'Story Of My Life' on Spanish version of The Voice and had most of the audience in tears!**

✈ It's rumoured the boys are planning to open a string of cafés across the globe, starting in Japan and then spreading to other major cities. 1D fairy cakes, anyone?

✈ **Zayn once cried on a German TV show when the band were presented with a scrap book some fans had made for the group. Bless!**

The lads reckon Japan is the best place to shop

The boys are popular across the globe

The band spend lots of time in hotels

A wave is universal!

# Quiz Answers

Are you a One Direction superfan or a superflop?
Find out how well you did in our 1D quiz!

## The Giant ID quiz

**1** Midnight Memories

**2** James

**3** Louis

**4** Harry

**5** What Makes You Beautiful

**6** Zayn

**7** Zayn

**8** Simon Cowell

**9** This Is Us

**10** Louis

**11** Chilled Eskimo

**12** Niall

**13** Harry

**14** Let Me Love You by Mario

**15** Nicole and Ruth

**16** Justin Beiber

**17** Louis

**18** Harry

**19** Harry

**20** Geoff

**21** Louis

**22** Four

**23** Bradford

**24** Niall

**25** Harry

**26** Liam

**27** Zayn

**28** Liam

**29** Three

**30** Harry

## Spot the difference

**1** Some of the writing is missing

**2** Harry's got nice new purple hair!

**3** Zayn's jeans have a bigger rip in them

**4** Liam's trousers have turned bright green!

**5** Niall's missing a bracelet

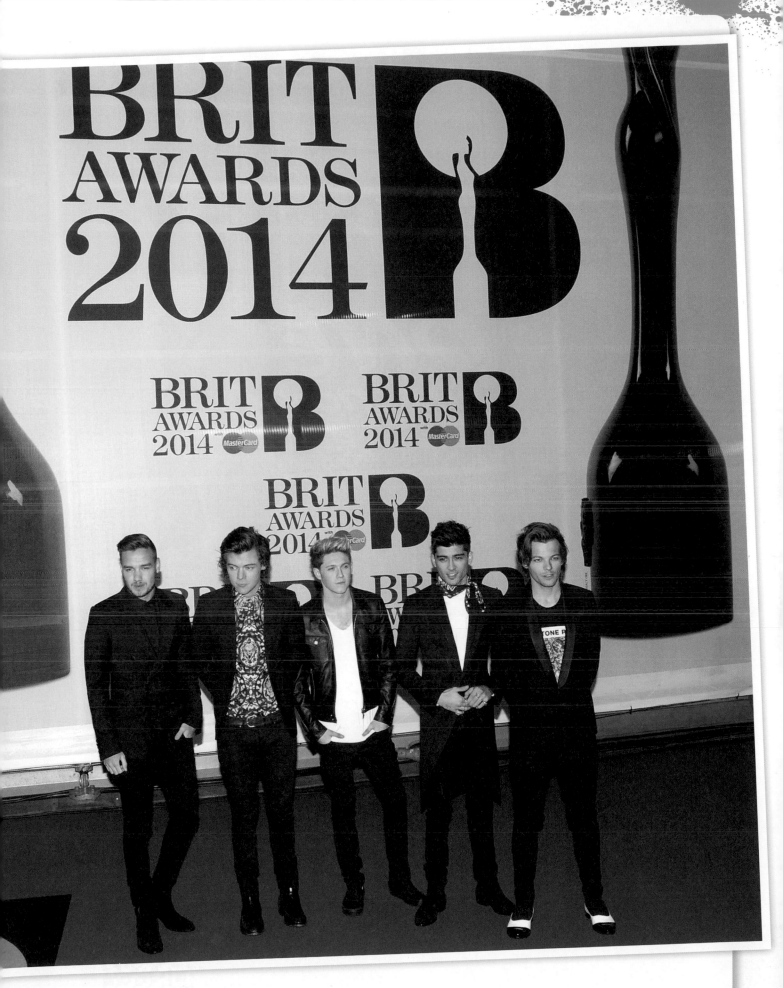